JAVA LAMBDAS AND PARALLEL STREAMS

Michael Müller

Apress®

Java Lambdas and Parallel Streams

Michael Müller
Brühl, Nordrhein-Westfalen,
Germany

ISBN-13 (pbk): 978-1-4842-2486-1   ISBN-13 (electronic): 978-1-4842-2487-8
DOI 10.1007/978-1-4842-2487-8

Library of Congress Control Number: 2016960327

Managing Director: Welmoed Spahr
Lead Editor: Steve Anglin
Technical Reviewer: Kishori Sharan
Editorial Board: Steve Anglin, Pramila Balan, Laura Berendson, Aaron Black,
    Louise Corrigan, Jonathan Gennick, Robert Hutchinson, Celestin Suresh John,
    Nikhil Karkal, James Markham, Susan McDermott, Matthew Moodie,
    Natalie Pao, Gwenan Spearing
Coordinating Editor: Mark Powers
Copy Editor: Deanna Hegle
Compositor: SPi Global
Indexer: SPi Global
Artist: SPi Global

To my wife Claudia and my kids:

Thank you for your patience during night-writing and other long sessions.

I love you.

To the many people I conversed with at conferences as well as attendees of my talks:

Thank you for the informative and interesting conversations. From that, I recognized how important the matter of Java Lambdas and Streams is for you and how much information demand exists. Without you, this book would not have been written.

To you, my dear reader:

Thank you for your interest in this book. I hope I wrote an understandable and valuable book, which helps you to achieve success.

Contents

About the Author.................................vii

About the Technical Reviewer.....................ix

Foreword...xi

Chapter 1:   Introduction 1

Chapter 2:   The Data.............................5

Chapter 3:   First Analysis—From Naive to Flexible 7

Chapter 4:   Lambda Expressions 13

Chapter 5:   Default Method 19

Chapter 6:   Optional 25

Chapter 7:   Make the Acquaintance of Streams 29

Chapter 8:   stream(), Stream and Spliterator.......35

Chapter 9:   Parallel Stream 41

Chapter 10: Collector and Concurrency 47

Chapter 11: GroupingCollector...................61

Appendix A: Program to Create the Demo Data 69

Index 85

About the Author

Michael Müller is an IT professional with more than 30 years of experience including, about 25 years in the health care sector. During this time, he has worked in different areas, especially project and product management, consulting, and software development. During a couple of software development projects, he also gained intensive international experience.

Currently, Michael is the head of software development at the German DRG institute inek.org. In this role, he is responsible for Web applications as well as other Java and .NET projects. Web projects are preferably built with Java technologies such as JSF (JavaServer Faces) with the help of supporting languages like JavaScript.

Michael has strong experience using lambda statements the .Net environment (LINQ with C#). Beginning with Java 8, he can finally use similar powerful features with Java.

Michael is a JSF professional user and a member of the Java Specification Request (JSR) 344 and JSR 372 (JSF) expert groups. His first book, *Web Development with Java and JSF* consequentially deals with this Java web technology.

He frequently reads books and writes reviews as well as technical papers, which are mostly published in German print magazines and on his web site.

About the Technical Reviewer

Kishori Sharan works as a software architect at Up and Running, Inc. He has earned a master of science degree in Computer Information Systems from Troy State University, Troy, Alabama. He is a Sun-certified Java 2 programmer. He has over 18 years of experience in developing enterprise applications and providing training to professional developers in the Java platform.

Foreword

Whenever I have spoken about Java Lambdas and Streams at conferences and roundtable events, there has been strong interest and lively discussions with the attendees. Typically, the unfamiliar syntax forms a significant hurdle even (or especially?) for experienced programmers. However, once a developer masters the syntax, she or he usually doesn't want to revert to the pre-lambda style.

Realizing that the new syntax is an impediment for many developers, I decided to share my experience and insights in a format that can be used as a reference. The aim of this concise book is to help you to overcome the learning curve and to master the new world of Lambdas and Streams.

Following Leanpub's motto "Publish Early, Publish Often", I published a previous edition in an early but complete state. This edition published by Apress contains additional information on how to create your own parallel collectors.

I hope that you enjoy reading it and achieve sustained success with Java Lambdas and Parallel Streams.

—Michael Müller
Brühl, Germany

Introduction

Lambdas and (Parallel) Streams

Some of the new features introduced in Java 8, such as the new Date and Time API (application program interfaces), feel quite familiar and can be used immediately by an experienced Java developer. But some of the most important enhancements, including Lambdas and Streams, require the developer to learn some new concepts. Lambda statements in particular introduce a syntax that is quite unusual for object-oriented programmers. These language constructs are known only to developers who used functional programming languages or enhancements like Microsoft's Linq (Language Integrated Query). This special syntax takes some getting used to, and some developers may even be a little frightened at first glance. However, these enhancements are extremely powerful, and it is certainly worth taking the time to understand how they can help you to write code that is not only concise but also faster to write and more reusable.

Electronic supplementary material The online version of this chapter (doi:10.1007/978-1-4842-2487-8_1) contains supplementary material, which is available to authorized users.

© Michael Müller 2016
M. Müller, *Java Lambdas and Parallel Streams*,
DOI 10.1007/978-1-4842-2487-8_1

In this book, I start with an explanation of Lambda expressions; show how they can be used with Streams; and finally, discuss how both Lambdas and Streams can be combined to implement effective parallel processing.

The following task will run like a golden thread through the book:

The Challenge

- Analyze a bigger amount of data according to varying criteria

- Parallelize this task without explicit use of thread management, synchronization, Excecutor, or ForkJoin

The Solution

Use parallelStream() instead of stream()!

A First Explanation

You may well ask, "what the hell are the stream() and parallelStream() methods?" Here is the quick overview; a more detailed description is given in later chapters.

You may imagine a Stream as a continuous flow of data, comparable to something like an InputStream. The data might be emitted by different sources, such as a collection, a file, a generator, or some other source. However, the content of this stream is not simply bytes or characters; instead, the stream emits arbitrary objects(see Figure 1-1).

Figure 1-1. Stream (quelle is German for source)

On their journey from source to target, the objects may be filtered, changed, transformed, collected, or processed in some other way. How and with whichever means this happens I describe later on.

A ParallelStream can be imagined as a parallel stream of objects of the same type. The objects are split into different streams at their source (see Figure 1-2). Later on, I will discuss the details of this splitting task.

Figure 1-2. Parallel streams

To implement solutions to the challenge, I will use some of Java's new language features, including

- Lambda statements
- Functional interfaces
- Default methods
- Optionals
- Streams
- Operations on streams

The Data

Back to the challenge.

I shall analyze data about a large number of persons who buy and sell diverse products. The data structure for this task has a simple design: A person has a given name, surname, age, and gender. A buyer might also be a vendor. Sales and purchases are stored in lists. Each element in this list represents a product by its article number, the quantity sold, and the unit price. The unit price may change per transaction due to various discounts. The following diagram (Figure 2-1) visualizes the class Person.

© Michael Müller 2016
M. Müller, *Java Lambdas and Parallel Streams*,
DOI 10.1007/978-1-4842-2487-8_2

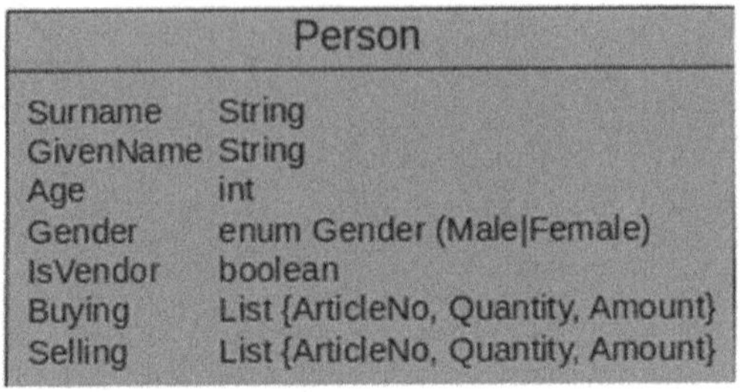

Person	
Surname	String
GivenName	String
Age	int
Gender	enum Gender (Male|Female)
IsVendor	boolean
Buying	List {ArticleNo, Quantity, Amount}
Selling	List {ArticleNo, Quantity, Amount}

Figure 2-1. Class Person

In the appendix, you'll find a simple program to create sample data.

First Analysis— From Naive to Flexible

In this section, I will develop traditional solutions to various filtering requirements. I avoid using Lambdas or Streams so that the techniques illustrated here can be compared with the solutions developed in Chapter 4.

© Michael Müller 2016
M. Müller, *Java Lambdas and Parallel Streams*,
DOI 10.1007/978-1-4842-2487-8_3

Fix Filter

The first task is to list all customers who are less than 20 years old. This can be done very easily; all we need is a loop with a filter condition to select young customers and a target list to collect them (see Listing 3-1).

Listing 3-1. *Simple Implementation to Select and Collect Persons Younger Than 20 Years*

```
1    private List<Person> getPersonsLessThan20Years(List
     <Person> persons){
2      List<Person> result = new ArrayList<>();
3      for (Person person : persons) {
4        if (person.getAge() < 20) {
5          result.add(person);
6        }
7      }
8      return result;
9    }
```

Simple Parameterization

The next requirement is to collect the group of people between 30 and 40 years old. Of course, we realize that in the future, we may need to query different age groups; so it would be better to parameterize the method rather than hard-coding the condition (see Listing 3-2).

Listing 3-2. *Parameterized Implementation to Choose All Persons of a Specified Age Group*

```
1    private List<Person> getPersonsByAgeRange(
2                                  List<Person> persons,
3                                  int from,
4                                  int to) {
5    List<Person> result = new ArrayList<>();
6      for (Person person : persons) {
```

```
7       if (person.getAge() >= from && person.getAge() <=
        to) {
8          result.add(person);
9       }
10    }
11    return result;
12  }
```

Here, the developer has introduced some flexibility. However, this method still does no more than select persons of a specified age group. If additional criteria are needed, such as querying the gender, this method doesn't help. A novice programmer might try to solve the problem by adding extra parameters for gender, vendor, status, and so forth (see Listing 3-3).

Listing 3-3. Overloading a Method with (Too) Many Parameters

```
1    private List<Person> getPersonsByDiverseCriteria(
2                                  List<Person> persons,
3                                  int ageFrom,
4                                  int ageTo,
5                                  Gender gender,
6                                  boolean isCustomer,
7                                  boolean isVendor) {
8      [loop omitted]
9    }
```

Senior developers might shake their heads at such naive code; their experience tells them that one day you won't be able to do your analysis because you will need at least one more parameter.

Behavior Parameterization

The next evolutionary step toward a better solution is to create the condition or filter as a stand-alone object and to pass it to the now more general-purpose method. This allows the method to be parameterized with different behaviors, or different algorithms, reminding us of the strategy pattern.

For our task, this behavior will implement an interface that contains a test to choose a person by a specified condition. Let's call this interface *Condition* (see Listing 3-4).

Listing 3-4. Interface Condition

```
1    public interface Condition<T> {
2      boolean test(T t);
3    }
```

Now our method (the loop) needs only two parameters: the list of persons and the condition (Listing 3-5).

Listing 3-5. Flexible Filtering Due to Injectable Condition

```
1    private List<Person> getPersonsByCondition(List<Person>
     persons, \
2
3                        Condition<Person> condition){
4      List<Person> result = new ArrayList<>();
5      for (Person person : persons) {
6        if (condition.test(person)) {
7          result.add(person);
8        }
9      }
10     return result;
11   }
```

The condition is swapped out and will be injected by a parameter. Thus, there is no need to change the implementation of the method when we need a different filter. Now let's refactor our first analysis to get everyone less than 20 years old (see Listing 3-6).

Listing 3-6. Implementation of the Condition According to Interface Condition

```
1    class YoungerThanCondition implements
     Condition<Person>{
2      private final int _age;
3      YoungerThanCondition(int age){
4        _age = age;
5      }
```

```
6
7     @Override
8     public boolean test(Person person) {
9       return person.getAge() < _age;
10    }
11  }
```

Now, the code to call our loop and to inject the filter looks more clean and concise (Listing 3-7).

Listing 3-7. *Call Loop with Filter*

```
1   persons = getPersonsByCondition(persons, new
    YoungerThanCondition(20));
```

Following the object-oriented paradigm, we pass the condition to the method as an object. Now, if we need other filter criteria, we simply create different filter classes as implementations of the *Condition* interface. The loop to collect the persons of interest remains unchanged.

Anonymous Classes

But creating a separate class for each different condition still seems to be a heavyweight approach. The question is this: "If we only need to use the condition in one place, can we create the class just where we'll need it?" This is where anonymous classes come into play (see Listing 3-8).

Listing 3-8. *Parameterize with Anonymous Class*

```
1   persons = getPersonsByCondition(persons, new
    Condition<Person>(){
2       @Override
3       public boolean test(Person person) {
4         return person.getAge() < 20;
5       }
6     });
```

Because the anonymous class is just created where it is needed, we can't reuse it. It doesn't make sense to pass the age as a parameter; we simply write it directly into the condition.

Compared with the fully fledged filter classes, anonymous classes are much shorter. But instead of passing a short class name as the parameter, we have to override the *test* method and to write a couple of lines. Anonymous classes are shorter than fully fledged classes but move the code into the parameter; this may not seem ideal. And by the way—lots of programmers dislike anonymous classes.

Lambda Expressions

After all of these traditional approaches, it's time to move on to the lambda expressions, which have been introduced into Java 8.

Just to remind you, the method `test()` of the interfaces *Condition* expects a *Person* and checks a condition.

Let's call this condition a function. Do you remember mathematics at school? Many pupils had to learn about functions and expressions such as $x \rightarrow f(x)$. This meant a value x will be mapped to a function of x. In our current task, a Person will be mapped to a function (Condition) of Person. And Java's lambda syntax reminds you exactly of this. For our concrete analysis, this will be as in Listing 4-1.

Listing 4-1. Lambda Expression for Age Condition

```
1    person -> person.getAge() < 20
```

© Michael Müller 2016
M. Müller, *Java Lambdas and Parallel Streams*,
DOI 10.1007/978-1-4842-2487-8_4

Now you can use this expression in place of the condition interface (see Listing 4-2).

Listing 4-2. Collect Persons with Lambda Expression

```
1    persons = getPersonsByCondition(
2                        persons,
3                        person -> person.getAge() < 20);
```

This is concise and clear code, easy to read and understand-able—once you are familiar with this syntax. Even (or especially?) for senior developers, the unusual syntax is often the biggest hurdle.

I predict that once a programmer has chummed up with it, he or she usually doesn't want to miss it anymore.

Finally it is possible to exchange the condition for our analysis in an easy way. The example in Listing 4-3 shows how to select all female persons.

Listing 4-3. Changing the Filter by Just a Lambda Expression

```
1    persons = getPersonsByCondition(
2    persons,
3    person -> person.getGender() == Gender.Female);
```

Functional Interface

Lambda expressions may be used where a functional interface is expected. We call an interface *functional interface* if it defines accurately one abstract method. The lambda expression overrides this method.

With Java 8, a couple of predefined functional interfaces are included (e.g., see Figure 4-1). Therefore, an extra definition such as the one we did with *Condition* is not needed. In our case, we could use the predefined interface *Predicate*, which is used to check such a condition. A list of the functional interfaces available with Java 8 can be read at Oracle.[1]

---

[1]https://docs.oracle.com/javase/8/docs/api/java/util/function/package-summary.html

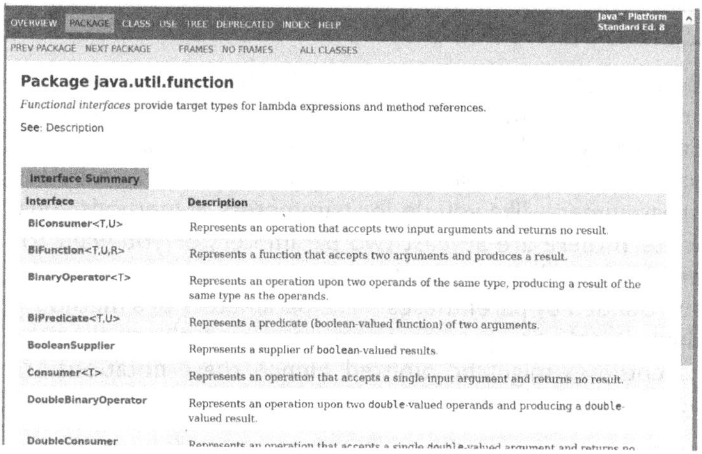

Figure 4-1. Predefined Functional Interfaces

These functional interfaces usually are annotated with @FunctionalInterface. This is an informative annotation and might be used by an IDE (integrated development environment) or by the compiler who is able to check the requirements of such an interface. However, for the usage with a lambda expression, this interface is not needed.

The functional interfaces defined with Java 8 mostly contains other useful concrete methods. A method implementation within an interface is a new feature of Java 8. These so called default methods are preconditions for extensions such as the new Stream API, and I will describe them later on.

Lambda Notation

Because of the interface that has to be implemented, the compiler has the ability to determine the count and the data types of the expected parameters. The names of the parameters don't matter and can be freely chosen by the programmer—like you do for parameters of methods you'll write. If there are at least two parameters or you want (or need to) declare a type, then the parameters need to be surrounded by parentheses—like parameters of a method. If there is only one parameter and no type declared, then the parentheses might be omitted. Hence, these notations are equivalent (see Listing 4-4).

Listing 4-4. Different Notations of a Lambda Expression

```
1    persons = getPersonsByCondition(persons, person ->
     person.getAge() < 20);
2    persons = getPersonsByCondition(persons, p -> p.getAge()
     < 20);
3    persons = getPersonsByCondition(persons, (Person p) ->
     p.getAge() < 20);
```

In detail, a lambda expression consists of a parameter list, the lambda operator "–>" (*minus + greater than* character), and a statement. As usual, this statement may be a block statement, which is built up by a couple of substatements.

```
(parameter list) -> statement
```

Here are the most important rules mentioned in brief: Type + name like method parameters in parentheses (`int x, int y) -> x * y;`

Clearly, determinable types might be omitted.

```
(x, y) -> x * y;
```

An empty parameter list is possible too and needs a pair of parentheses.

```
() -> getVendorCount(persons)
```

If there is only one parameter without any type declaration, the parentheses might be omitted.

```
x -> x * x;
```

As special notations, lambda expressions may be replaced by a so-called method or object references.

- `class::method`
- `object::method`

Let's take a look at the class *Person*. This contains a boolean method `isVendor()`. If this is needed in a condition, then the lambda expression would be

```
p -> p.isVendor()
```

Using a method reference instead will change the code too.

```
Person::isVendor
```

Observe the discontinuance of the parentheses. Using a method reference sometimes can lead to a more concise notation. I mention it here for completeness. Later on in this book, I use it rarely and without further explanation. Detailed information about this matter is available, for example, in the Java tutorials.[2]

Lazy Evaluation

You may treat a lambda expression as a kind of function reference. And this function is not executed at the time you assign it to a variable but only when evaluating the variable. This lazy evaluation might be used to realize an around-invoke. For example, we may push the evaluation into a method that measures the execution time.

---

[2]`https://docs.oracle.com/javase/tutorial/java/java00/methodreferences.html`

In the following snippet, getVendorCount will be executed immediately.

```
int personCount = getVendorCount(persons);
```

Using a lambda expression, it is simple to pass getVendor-Count as a function into a different method.

```
int personCount = invokeMethod(() ->
getVendorCount(persons));
```

The essential part is that getVendorCount will not be executed here. It will be carried out within the measuring method, just when method.get() is called (Listing 4-5).

Listing 4-5. Messfunktion zum Aufruf einer Methode

```
1    private static <T> T invokeMethod(Supplier<T> method) {
2       long start = System.nanoTime();
3       T result = method.get();
4       long elapsedTime = System.nanoTime() - start;
5       System.out.println("Elapsed time: " +
         elapsedTime/1000000);
6       return result;
7    }
```

Summary

Using lambda expressions, we were successful in implementing a flexible filter function for the data.

However, we can only change the filter condition so far. If we need to use a different kind of evaluation, for example, amount and total price of an article, we still need to adapt the method. Here, the stream interface comes into play, which allows you to do without the loop and to chain other execution steps such as transformation or reduction. To understand how Java could be enhanced by this interface, we first need to introduce some other new Java features. One of these enhancements is the chance to create default methods. I will show this within Chapter 5.

Default Method

The Problem

An interface might be treated as a kind of contract between a provider and a user. As such, it can't be recalled or changed unilaterally. If you develop software against an interface, you must rely on the function. If the provider (e.g., developer of a framework) changes the interface, it might be possible that your software can't use the new version anymore. If you are in luck, your compiled program may still work together with the new version. This is the case if the change keeps binary compatibility. By the next time you need to compile your program, the compiler usually reports an error: the compiler forces all methods of the interface to be implemented. Because the changed interface is not source compatible, you need to adopt your program.

So how can you enhance an interface without breaking source and binary compatibility?

© Michael Müller 2016
M. Müller, *Java Lambdas and Parallel Streams*,
DOI 10.1007/978-1-4842-2487-8_5

Solution—The Java Way

The developers of the Java language solved this problem by introducing *default methods*. These are concrete method implementations within the interface, declared as `default`. If none of the existing parts are changed, an interface that has been enhanced by default methods can be used directly by all classes that implement it: without the need to change these implementing classes!

Because a default method is a ready to use method, there is no need to implement it, and the enhanced interface keeps source and binary compatibility. Beginning with Java 8, your classes may use methods from parent classes as well as from interfaces. Thus, Java virtual has a kind of multiple inheritance or mixin now.

What about the (well-) known problems of multiple inheritance? Or what happens if your class or a parent class of it already possesses a method of the same name and signature?

Java 8 has a couple of well-defined rules to prevent problems that are described in the following. For simplification, we now call it "homonymous" methods if we discuss methods of the same name and signature.

- If the (abstract) method signatures of the enhanced interface stay unchanged, the interface will be source and binary compatible

- The interface might be enhanced by concrete methods, which are available for inheritance

- If the implementing class contains a homonymous method, this has priority

- The interface provider is able to enhance the interface

- Enhancements of implemented libraries by the library user are not possible (enhancements by the provider only)

- This is in contrast to extension methods of other languages, which enhance existing classes by the user

- There are well-defined rules to choose the right method in case of homonymous implementation

- Fields ("member" variables) defined in an interface are implicit final

- Despite these restrictions, default methods have a great potential

- Best examples are the stream() and parallelStream() methods not only of the Java 8 collections

Rules to Choose a Default Method

Java 8 defines some rules for which method will be used in case of homonymous methods. If it can't be decided, the compiler will report an error.

As the name *default method* implies, this method is only used as a default if no implementation is used in the implementing class. If there are homonymous methods in different interfaces the class will implement, the compiler will choose the method that is "closest" to the class. This is independent from the fact of whether theses interfaces are derived from each other or are independent.

The following examples will demonstrate this (see Listings 5-1 to 5-3).

Listing 5-1. Interface with Default Method

```
1   public interface InterfaceA {
2     default void print (){
3        System.out.println("InterfaceA");
4     }
5   }
```

Listing 5-2. Implementing Class (Without Further Functionality)

```
1   public class InterfaceImplementor implements
InterfaceA{}
```

Listing 5-3. Invocation of the Class

```
1   public class InterfaceDemo {
2       public static void main(String[] args) {
3          new InterfaceImplementor().print();
4       }
5   }
```

Create a Java project using these three files to comprehend the operating mode.

As you may have expected, this small demo simply prints out InterfaceA. The a next interface with a homonymous method will be added (see Listing 5-4).

Listing 5-4. InterfaceB with Homonymous Default Method

```
1   public interface InterfaceB {
2     default void print (){
3        System.out.println("InterfaceB");
4     }
5   }
```

Last but not least, the class InterfaceImplementor needs to implement this additional interface (Listing 5-5).

Listing 5-5. *Implementing Class (Without Further Functionality)*

```
1   public class InterfaceImplementor implements InterfaceA,
    InterfaceB{}
```

A modern IDE will alert an error (see Figure 5-1).

```
Source  History
1   package de.muellerbruehl.parallelstreams.interfaces;
2
@   public class InterfaceImplementor implements InterfaceA, InterfaceB{}
4
```

Figure 5-1. NetBeans alerts misusage

In either case, the compiler will tell you that it can't compile this program. What will happen if you create inheritance with these interfaces?

In the case of the preceding example, it is possible to inherit from InterfaceA and/or InterfaceB. As long as you use two different interfaces in your implementing class, which have different homonymous default methods, the compiler will alert an error.

It becomes a bit different if the interfaces inherit from a common interface that has such a default method. Create two interfaces that both inherit from InterfaceA. One of them will override the default method. For brevity, these three files are shown as one listing (Listing 5-6).

Listing 5-6. *Inheritance of Default Method*

```
1   public interface InterfaceA11 {
2     default void print (){
3       System.out.println("InterfaceA11");
4     }
5   }
6
7   public interface InterfaceA12 {}
8
9   public class InterfaceImplementor implements
    InterfaceA11, InterfaceA12{}
```

If you run this program, it will print out *InterfaceA11*. The print method of `InterfaceA11` resides on the lowest level of the inheritance hierarchy. Thus, it is "closest" to the implementing class. The same is valid if you implement interfaces from different hierarchic levels.

```
public class InterfaceImplementor implements InterfaceA,
InterfaceA11{}
```

This will call the print method from `InterfaceA11` too.

If you want to program and use two homonymous methods on the same level, for example, develop a print method in `InterfaceA12` too, the compiler can't determine which to choose and reports an error.

Summary

Default methods enable the enhancement of existing interfaces without breaking compatibility. In this sense, they build the foundation for new features like stream(), which I describe later on. Before, I have to discuss another enhancement: the Optional class.

Read further descriptions of default methods in the Internet, for example, at Oracle.[1]

---

[1] `https://docs.oracle.com/javase/tutorial/java/IandI/defaultmethods.html`

Optional

First of all, we take a look at another family of classes that play their role in using the new streams: Optional.

As you know, if you declare but do not initialize an object in Java, its value is null. If you try to access a method of an object with value of null, you'll get a null pointer exception. Sadly, we cannot avoid a null value at any time. At least we need a something to represent the absence of an object. To avoid null pointer exceptions, you need to check many places within your software diverse variables for a null value (see Listing 6-1).

Listing 6-1. Check for Non-Null Value

```
1   String name;
2   [...]
3   if (name != null) {...}
```

Java 8 introduced the class Optional, which encapsulates an optional object and offers methods to check the content (Listing 6-2).

© Michael Müller 2016
M. Müller, *Java Lambdas and Parallel Streams*,
DOI 10.1007/978-1-4842-2487-8_6

Listing 6-2. Check for Presence

```
1   Optional<String> name;
2   [...]
3   if (name.isPresent()){...}
```

At first glance, this looks like replacing one evil with another. Still, there are the same amount of checks, not for null but for presence. And an additional class is required. So where is the excess profit

The class Optional offers a bit more than just simple tests for presence. First of all, you may tell this class which exception to throw in case of the absence of the encapsulated object. Replacing the dumb null pointer exception by one of your choice in conjunction with a detailed message is a great plus in case of error. On the other hand, Optional offers some methods to retrieve a value.

To access the encapsulated object, you use the method get(). And with orElse() you specify an alternative, which is used in case of an absence value. This prevents you from any "no value exception" and allows you to develop your software with less checks.

You'll find more details about Optional within the API documentation.[1]

At the beginning of this chapter, I talked about a family of classes. Optional is a single class that is directly derived from Object. Besides that, there are the classes OptionalDouble, OptionalInt, OptionalLong, which are directly derived from Object too. These classes have a similar behavior to Optional. Thus, this class family is neither defined by inheritance from a common parent nor by implementing a common interface. These classes are simply programmed in a similar way and implement a behavior that is close together.

---

[1]https://docs.oracle.com/javase/8/docs/api/java/util/Optional.html

There are slightly different methods. For example, to retrieve the value of an optional Double, the method is not get() but getAsDouble()—and we use it when we learn about Streams in Chapter 7.

Make the Acquaintance of Streams

Ok, back to the analysis of the data.

Let's assume two existing filters can't be combined to one complex condition but have to be applied one after the other. Or we need separate steps to transform the data, or, or, . . .

Generally speaking, the data will be processed in a chain. Each operation takes some data, performs any kind of operation, and produces an intermediate result, which is used as input for the next task. Such a procedure is known as pipelining (see Figure 7-1).

© Michael Müller 2016
M. Müller, *Java Lambdas and Parallel Streams*,
DOI 10.1007/978-1-4842-2487-8_7

Figure 7-1. Classical process chain

Operations work differently when using a stream. All transformations in the chain are performed "on the fly." From the developers point of view, there is a data input at the beginning of the chain and one output at its end, but no explicit intermediate result (Figure 7-2).

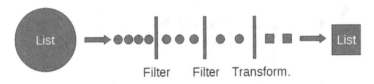

Figure 7-2. Stream prosessing

The developer needs to create a data source and then appends the processing steps till the last one. This so-called terminal operation creates the result. The data flow only starts when the final operation is invoked.

The trick is an internal iterator, which emits the data. Due to this, there is no need for the programmer to create a loop (which is nothing else but an external iterator). The developer just needs to tell the system how to handle the data. The former loop now looks like a serial process—which can be parallelized in an easy way later on.

Examples

To get a first impression of how the Stream works, we take a look at a couple of use cases. It doesn't matter whether you do not understand everything right now—later on I will discuss the details (see Listing 7-1).

Listing 7-1. *List All Female Persons with Age Below 20*

```
1   List<Person> youngFemales = persons.stream()
2   .filter(p -> p.getAge() < 20)
3   .filter(p -> p.isFemale())
4   .collect(Collectors.toList());
```

The code person.stream() emits all data as a stream using an internal iterator. Lines 2 and 3 (Listing 7-1) act as two chained filters; and in the last line, the resulting data is collected into a list. I will discuss collect() and Collectors later on.

Listing 7-2. *Average Age of All Females Younger Than 20*

```
1   double averageAge = persons.stream()
2                   .filter(p -> p.getAge() < 20 &&
                    p.isFemale())
3                   .mapToInt(Person:p -> p.getAge())
4                   .average()
5                   .getAsDouble();
```

In Listing 7-2, we first filter for the same persons as in Listing 7-1. For a little variation, the condition is realized as a combined one. Because this has no noticeable affect on performance, the first variant might be preferable, especially because it is possible to combine the single processing steps dynamically at runtime.

In line 3 of Listing 7-2, we have a mapping, which takes an object of the stream (Person) and yields a different one: the stream will continue with the person's age. Next, we calculate the average of it. At the end of the process chain, we'll get the result from type Double and assign it to the variable on the left side (averageAge on line 1).

Listing 7-3. *Total Count of Selling*

```
1   long totalSelling = persons
2           .stream()
3           .filter(Person::isVendor)
4           .mapToLong(p -> p.getSelling().values()
5                   .stream()
```

```
6                     .mapToLong(ArticleInfo::getQuantity)
7                     .sum())
8           .sum();
```

Just to remind you, all data is available as a list of persons. Some of them are labeled as vendors. For each vendor, all selling is stored in a list.

In Listing 7-3, the total count of selling is calculated. With a traditional approach, you would implement two loops: one loop to iterate the persons and the inner one to iterate through the selling.

By streams, it is realized with two loops also, but these loops are hidden to the developer. The code reads like a serial process: take all persons, determine the vendors, and for each calculate the amount (lines 4–7) and then the final sum. This is clear and concise code—and maybe unfamiliar. But once you know the lambda syntax and internal iterators, it becomes easy to read. Could you have made it shorter without lambdas and streams?

If you don't like the duplicate call of the sum function, we can realize the calculation in a different way. It is possible to flatten the "stream of streams." For this, Java offers `flatMap`, or in this concrete solution, a `flatMapToLong` (Listing 7-4).

Listing 7-4. *Total Count of Selling with Flattened Stream*

```
1   long totalSelling = persons
2           .stream()
3           .filter(Person::isVendor)
4           .flatMapToLong(p -> p.getSelling().values().
            stream()
5           .mapToLong(ArticleInfo::getQuantity))
6           .sum();
```

As the examples show, the stream interfaces comes along with a fluent API. You may combine all methods via dot notation. Thus, the processing looks more declarative: you describe what will happen to your data. For processing, we have to distinguish intermediate from terminal operations.

An intermediate operation is one that is processed within the stream. Examples for these are filter, map, or sorted. They accept a stream and emit one.

A terminal operation closes the stream. Examples for this kind of operation are collect, reduce, and sum. Understandably, there can be only one terminal operation.

The process does not start until the terminal operation is called. Thus, a stream realizes the concept of lazy evaluation.

We can use this behavior to assign the intermediate steps to a variable and build the chain dynamically. The following code illustrates this concept; someCondition() and someOther-Condition() are placeholders for any condition.

Imagine a user interface where the user selects some combo boxes, check boxes, and other elements that are used to build up the processing. In real applications, you'll meet such simple, up to complex, builders (Listing 7-5).

Listing 7-5. Dynamic Build of Process Chain

```
1    Stream<Person> stream = persons.stream();
2    if (someCondition()){
3      stream = stream.filter(Person::isFemale);
4    }
5    if (someOtherCondition()){
6      stream = stream.filter(p -> p.getAge() < 20);
7    }
8    double average = stream
9            .mapToInt(p -> p.getAge())
10           .average()
11           .getAsDouble();
```

Parallel Processing

Parallelize   Using the last example (or any other), replace stream() by parallelStream(). Measure the time that is needed both for the sequential well as for the parallel variant on a multicore machine.

For taking the time, you can use the method invokeMethod, which was introduced in Chapter 4 (see Listing 7-6).

Listing 7-6. *Measure Time*

```
1   Supplier<Long> totalSelling = () ->
2           persons.stream()
3           .filter(Person::isVendor)
4           .flatMapToLong(p -> p.getSelling().values().
            stream()
5           .mapToLong(ArticleInfo::getQuantity))
6           .sum();
7   System.out.println("total: " +
    invokeMethod(totalSelling));
```

As stated at the beginning of this book in the section *The Solution* (Chapter 1), it is really possible to *realize parallel processing by the usage of* parallelStream() *in place of* stream(). Although this looks quite simple, you have to consider some ancillary conditions. I will further investigate this.

Summary

With the default method stream(), Java 8 offers an enhancement of the collection framework as well as other interfaces without breaking compatibility. It offers you an apparently sequential programming of solutions that need a loop under the hood. Above all, it is possible to parallelize by replacing this method by parallelStream().

In this chapter, the streams had been preponderantly introduced by concise examples. After this first overview, it's time to dive into some details. I will focus especially on the interfaces Stream and Spliterator.

stream(), Stream and Spliterator

By now, you have a first impression how you can use `stream()` and `parallelStream()`. We want to look behind the scenes and investigate these methods further.

Investigate the implementation in Java. Find out how you can display the Java source code within your IDE. In the case of NetBeans,[1] simply open one of the preceding examples and place the cursor onto `stream()`. Using the key combination {Ctrl+B} invokes the `goto` source code.

[1]http://netbeans.org

© Michael Müller 2016
M. Müller, *Java Lambdas and Parallel Streams*,
DOI 10.1007/978-1-4842-2487-8_8

stream() and parallelStream() are default methods of the interface Collection (see Listing 8-1).

Listing 8-1. *Excerpt of the Interface* Collection

```
1   default Stream<E> stream() {
2      return StreamSupport.stream(spliterator(), false);
3   }
4
5   default Stream<E> parallelStream() {
6      return StreamSupport.stream(spliterator(), true);
7   }
```

As you can see, both methods are very similar. Both call StreamSupport.stream(). The only difference is the second parameter. This boolean parameter parallel might be false or true. Thus, it becomes clear why you can exchange both methods in many situations.

Both methods return a stream, which is defined by the interface Stream. And they use a so-called Spliterator, which is called via spliterator(). I discuss both within the next paragraphs.

Stream

The interface Stream defines a lot of methods that return a stream. They do not take the whole input to produce a full stream but element by element. As an example, let's take a look at the signature of filter:

```
Stream<T> filter(Predicate<? super T> predicate);
```

This produces a stream according to the filter condition. It is great to recognize that `filter` takes an element from type T[2] (or from its super class), which is an element of the stream. As shown before, `Predicate` is a functional interface. Hence, a lambda expression can be used to implement the predicate. Because the type is well known from the stream, the lambda expression has no need to declare the type. See previously in paragraph Rules for lambda expressions.

As shown with `filter`, `Stream` defines the way the intermediate operates. The type of emitted element might differ from the input (e.g., `map`). The output of a mapping operation is a stream of objects whose type can differ from the input. For example, we may map a person to his or her age or name.

For some data types, there are special streams defined. For example, there are Long or Double streams, which support additional mathematical operations. And within `Stream`, some intermediate operations are defined to convert to such a special stream. In the previous examples, we used `.mapTo-Long(...)`, which performs such a mapping for a predefined stream type.

```
LongStream mapToLong(ToLongFunction<? super T> mapper);
```

`LongStream` isn't derived from `Stream`, but both are derived from `BaseStream`.

Besides intermediate operations, the Stream interfaces offer terminal operations as well as the generation of a stream.

Terminal operations are not only simple or complex "results" such as `min`, `max`, `collect` (which collects data, e.g., into a list) but the explicit call of a method for each element.

---

[2]If you do not know the common type notation of generics, take a look into the Internet, for example, at Wikipedia: de.wikipedia.org/wiki/Generische_Programmierung_in_Java or Oracle's Java Tutorial: docs.oracle.com/javase/tutorial/java/generics/methods.html.

```
void forEach(Consumer<? super T> action);
```

By forEach, the internal iterator is made available to a method that implements the interface Consumer. This is another functional interface too.

Let's take a look into terminal operations. The operation min, for example, usually yields the minimal value of a numeric stream. What happens if the stream does not contain any value? The result must be empty. And to avoid a null result, all those kind of operations produce an optional of the expected type. This result is not of type T, but of Optional<T>.

To describe all methods that are provided by Stream would go far beyond the scope of this concise book. The intention is to provide a good understanding of the principles. It is recommended to read the API documentation,[3] which is available using the URL in footnote 3 (valid at the time of this writing).

Spliterator

The Spliterator is responsible in splitting the object stream into smaller parts. Its name is short for "splitting iterator." This is the internal iterator mentioned several times. Besides iteration, the splitting part enables you to provide parts of the stream to different threads,

You can use a spliterator for sequential as well as parallel processing. Java 8 comes with a default implementation (see Listing 8-2).

Listing 8-2. Default Method Spliterator

```
1    @Override
2    default Spliterator<E> spliterator() {
3        return Spliterators.spliterator(this, 0);
4    }
```

---

[3]https://docs.oracle.com/javase/8/docs/api/java/util/stream/Stream.html

For special use cases, it is possible to create your own split-erator. Although in most cases, the existing implementation fits, it is very useful to understand the basic concepts.

The interface `Spliterator` defines two important methods.

```
boolean tryAdvance(Consumer<? super T> action);
```

The preceding code tries to execute an operation for the next element—if there is any. If it advanced successfully, this method returns `true` whereas `false` indicates the absence of an element (which is the end of the stream). This is a significant difference to the common iterator concept: Using an iterator, you first have to check whether at least one more element exists. If this `hasNext()` returns `true`, you can get it with `next()`.

The element `tryAdvance` has a companion that iterates thru the remaining elements. The second significant method is the following.

```
Spliterator<T> trySplit();
```

This tries to split the data in a meaningful way. If the size of the underlying data structure is well known, for example, if the data is held in an array, then `trySplit` splits into two halves of (nearly) the same size: `trySplit` returns an additional spliterator, which might divide the data again if needed. By this, the whole dataset would be split into a multitude of smaller datasets, which potentially could be processed in parallel.

If the amount of data is unknown, for example, because you read data from a file or receive it online by some data channel, then the split is performed by other criteria. For example, a file could be split after each 1,024 lines.

Although `tryAdvance` and `trySplit` are the most important methods in understanding the behavior of the spliterators, this interface offers many more methods and fields. If needed, you may read about that within the API documentation.[4]

---

[4]https://docs.oracle.com/javase/8/docs/api/java/util/Spliterator.html

Summary

The interface Stream defines a lot of methods to process data within a stream. Intermediate operations perform an action and yield another stream. This allows you to chain processing steps by a dot notation (fluent API).

The Spliterator is the internal Iterator, which is able to split the data into smaller chunks. This enables the parallel processing of these chunks. Sometimes you have to consider some constraints to enable a successful parallelization. I will discuss this in Chapter 9.

Parallel Stream

If by the usage of `parallelStream` the data can be processed correctly in parallel, you need to consider some ancillary conditions. In case of inobservance, either Java will prohibit parallel execution or you might get unexpected results.

- Use stateless lambda expressions.

  State means you keep a value somewhere, for instance, in a variable. Now, if a future execution of the lambda expression depends on this value, the behavior of parallel execution may become non-deterministic. The result potentially becomes nonpredictable. If you're lucky, the compiler prevents parallelism. Otherwise you will wonder about the results.

© Michael Müller 2016
M. Müller, *Java Lambdas and Parallel Streams*,
DOI 10.1007/978-1-4842-2487-8_9

- Do not change the data the stream is based on.

  For example, if you add or remove elements of a collection while iterating through it, it may work when you process sequential. Such code is not healthy and often leads to an exception. With a parallel stream, you can't use such poor code: you'll always get an exception.

- Avoid side effects.

  This is the main principle of functional programming. A function always returns the same result when the same parameters are provided. Side effects like changing a variable with broader scope should be avoided. If you are working with streams and like to use a variable with broader scope, the compiler will accept this only if these variables are used in the same manner as final variables. A modern IDE such as NetBeans would give you the advice that variables referenced from a lambda expression must be final or used effectively final.

- Processing must be independent from order.

  Because in the case of parallel processing, the order is not determined, it is essential that the result does not depend on the processing order. Or you need to enforce an ordered processing. This creates some overhead, which might consume the time you've earned with parallelism.

The problem of a calculation that depends on a special order can be investigated by the following example. The apparently same calculation is implemented in three different ways. To reproduce the stable or changing results, every variant is invoked multiple times.

Listing 9-1. Sequential, parallel and parallel ordered processing

```
1   long[] result = new long[1];
2
3   for (int i = 0; i < 10; i++) {
4     result[0] = 0;
5     LongStream.range(0, 1000)
6         .forEach(n -> result[0] = (result[0] + n) * n);
7     System.out.println("serial: " + result[0]);
8   }
9
10  for (int i = 0; i < 10; i++) {
11    result[0] = 0;
12    LongStream.range(0, 1000).parallel()
13        .forEach(n -> result[0] = (result[0] + n) * n);
14    System.out.println("parallel: " + result[0]);
15  }
16
17  for (int i = 0; i < 10; i++) {
18    result[0] = 0;
19    LongStream.range(0, 1000).parallel()
20        .forEachOrdered(n -> result[0] = (result[0] +
          n) * n);
21    System.out.println("parallel ordered: " + result[0]);
22  }
```

The stream is generated by range as LongStream. This delivers numbers in the desired range. There is no parallel-Stream as in the Collection interface, but you can switch to parallel processing by parallel().

The sequential variant as well as the ordered parallel one always report the result of *300375547974850215*, whereas the unordered parallel version creates different results.

The calculation of result[0] = (result[0] + n) * n) depends on the order. It's very clear that a zero in place of n will produce as zero as the next intermediate result (and a zero as final if processed last). Because the zero will be used at any time, you can't predict the result. If you further investigate the math, it becomes clear that it depends on the order for any other value too.

For a simple demonstration, these three demos use a side effect. All intermediate results will be stored in an external variable. Because this has to be effectively final, we used a dirty trick: instead of a long, we used an array.

In a productive application, never use such dirty tricks! Here is a clean variant.

```
1   long reduce = LongStream.range(0, 1000).reduce(0, (a, c)
-> (a + c) * c);
```

For those who are unfamiliar with lambdas, this looks very strange, while the dirty solution seems to be more understandable. That's why I used it for this demonstration. Never fear the clean solution. After using lambdas for a short while, this kind of programming is quite easy.

Here is a short explanation of the terminal reduce operation. The first parameter is used to initialize an accumulator. The second operation is a binary Function that takes the accumulator (a) and the current object (c) of the stream. The result of this operation will replace the former value of the accumulator and becomes available for the next object of the stream.

- By using Collect respect Concurrent

```
1  Map<Integer, List<Person>> ageMap = persons
2   .stream()
3   .collect(Collectors. groupingBy(Person::getAge));
4
5  ConcurrentMap<Integer, List<Person>> ageMapPar = persons
6   .parallelStream()
7   .collect(Collectors.groupingByConcurrent(Person::get
     Age));
```

- The collecting structure (here: Concurrent Map) may have the characteristics Collector.Character and Collector. Characteristics.UNORDERED.

Summary

Although parallel programming with streams is available without explicit thread handling and often without synchronization, you still have to consider some constraints to get correct results. Next, we'll examine the collect method with respect to Java concurrency.

Collector and Concurrency

So far, we have used the collect() method without further explanation. This overloaded method either takes a Collector, as we did before (e.g., .collect(Collectors.toList() or .collect(Collectors.groupingByConcurrent(Person::getAge))); or you may pass three arguments for supplier, accumulator, and combiner. Don't get puzzled yet; I'm going to explain these soon.

As its name suggests, the main purpose of collect is to collect data. This is done by modifying a mutable data structure. In contrast to this, the reduce() method applies to immutable data structures.

© Michael Müller 2016
M. Müller, *Java Lambdas and Parallel Streams*,
DOI 10.1007/978-1-4842-2487-8_10

Now it's time to write our own collector. For the sake of simplicity, we create a collector to sum up a stream of numbers. These numbers are generated by a simple number generator (Listing 10-1).

Listing 10-1. Number Generator

```
1   public static List<Long> createNumbers() {
2     List<Long> numbers = new ArrayList<>();
3     Random random = new Random();
4     int max = 1000000 + random.nextInt(1000000);
5     for (int i = 0; i < max; i++) {
6       numbers.add((long)random.nextInt(100));
7     }
8     return numbers;
9   }
```

But first of all, we take a quick look at Java concurrency. Although parallelStreams() avoids all the manual thread handling, a basic knowledge is useful to understand how to write a collector that successfully performs in parallel.

Java Concurrency

There are two terms we have to talk about: "concurrency" and "parallelism." We have to define both terms before we move on because we talk about Java concurrency, but parallel streams.

With concurrency, several parts of a program will be executed in different threads, running concurrent instead of serial. This does not necessarily imply that these threads run at the same time. Remember the old days of one single core CPU (central processing unit) per computer: to keep the user interface (ui) fluent, it had been a good practice to perform the ui handling in one thread and the time-consuming computation in a different one. Both threads alternating gained small slices of CPU time. On a modern multicore CPU, these threads may run in parallel.

On the other hand, within parallelism, a couple of parallel running threads would perform the same computation of different data simultaneously. Parallel streams implement parallelism. Take a look at the drawing (Figure 10-1): the parallel streams contain different data of the same type. Each intermediate operation is defined once and will be executed in parallel as suggested by the vertical alignment.

Figure 10-1. Parallel stream with intermediate operations

People may consider parallelism as a special case of concurrency or as something different. In this book, we won't deepen this discussion. Anyway, to get parallelism using Java, we technically need concurrency.

ℹ Processes and Threads Within this book we only deal with threads, which are separate units of a program, running within the same process. Whereas a process offers a completely separated environment with its own memory, threads run within a shared environment and especially share their memory. This fact becomes important if classes are used by multiple threads.

Get a more detailed explanation by the Java Tutorial.[1]

Java had been designed for multithreading from the very beginning. The class Thread has been part of Java since JDK (Java Development Kit) 1.0.

---

[1]`https://docs.oracle.com/javase/tutorial/essential/concurrency/procthread.html`

Let's take a look at how to define and run a second thread (Listing 10-2).

Listing 10-2. Simple Usage of Thread

```
1   public static void main(String[] args) {
2     Thread thread = new MyThread();
3     thread.start();
4     System.out.println("Message from Main");
5   }
6
7   private static class MyThread extends Thread {
8     @Override
9     public void run() {
10      System.out.println("Message from MyThread");
11    }
12  }
```

We simply need to define a class that is derived from Thread and overwrite the `run()` method. In the main program, we create a new instance of out thread and call `start()`. Behind the scenes, start requests a new thread from the operating system and performs the run method within this new thread.

But there is one problem. Usually you want to build up class structures by deriving them from a technical class and not from Thread. Fortunately, Java offers an alternative way to create a thread. We need to implement the interface Runnable. And that is exactly what the class Thread does internally (Listing 10-3).

Listing 10-3. Thread Using Runnable

```
1   public static void main(String[] args) {
2     Thread thread = new Thread(new MyRunnable());
3     thread.start();
4     System.out.println("Message from Main");
5   }
6
7   private static class MyRunnable implements Runnable {
8     @Override
```

```
 9      public void run() {
10        System.out.println("Message from MyRunnable");
11      }
12    }
```

Now, a new Thread is created by passing an object of our class. Everything else stays unchanged.

Armed with this knowledge, we want to use threads to perform the summing task. We create a class *SummingUnit*, which performs the calculation (Listing 10-4).

Listing 10-4. *SummingUnit*

```
 1    public class SummingUnit {
 2      public SummingUnit(){
 3        System.out.println("ctor SummingUnit");
 4      }
 5
 6      private long _sum = 0;
 7
 8      public long getSum() {
 9        return _sum;
10      }
11
12      public void sum(long value) {
13        _sum += value;
14      }
15
16      public void combine(SummingUnit other) {
17        _sum += other._sum;
18      }
19
20    }
```

This class internally uses a field to sum the values, which are passed to sum(). A simple getter is used to read the sum. The method combine() is initially not used; we need it later on. Remember the combiner argument of *collect*?

For demonstration, a new thread will process half of our number, whereas the other half is processed by the "main" part. To achieve this goal, I created *SumTask*, which takes the appropriate parameters for the first and second half. One instance of this class is called by a new thread and the other directly. To synchronize both threads, the main thread waits by thread. join until the spawned thread is finished (Listing 10-5).

Listing 10-5. *Parallel Summing—with Unexpected Results*

```
1   public static void main(String[] args) throws
    InterruptedException {
2     List<Long> numbers = Utils.createNumbers();
3     int size = numbers.size();
4     SummingUnit summingUnit = new SummingUnit();
5
6     Thread thread = new Thread(new SumTask(numbers, 0,
7             size / 2, summingUnit));
8     thread.start();
9
10    SumTask sumTask = new SumTask(numbers, size / 2,
11            size, summingUnit);
12    sumTask.run();
13    thread.join(); // wait for thread to complete
14
15    System.out.printlnJava concurrencyparallel
      summing("Sum: " + summingUnit.getSum());
16  }
17
18
19  private static class SumTask implements Runnable {
20
21    private final List<Integer> _numbers;
22    private final int _start;
23    private final int _end;
24    private final SummingUnit _summingUnit;
25
26    public SumTask(List<Integer> numbers,
27                        int start,
28                        int end,
29                        SummingUnit summingUnit) {
```

```
30        _numbers = numbers;
31        _start = start;
32        _end = end;
33        _summingUnit = summingUnit;
34      }
35
36      @Override
37      public void run() {
38        for (int i = _start; i < _end; i++) {
39          _summingUnit.sum(_numbers.get(i));
40        }
41      }
42    }
```

However, if you invoke this program a couple of times, you'll get different results, even though you wait for the second thread to finish. What happened?

Watch out for the sum() method.

```
sum += val;
```

At first glance, this looks like a single operation. But in fact, this is only syntactic sugar, and we can rewrite this statement.

```
sum = sum + val;
```

With our common hardware structure, it is not possible to perform an addition within a variable. In fact, the computer must load the value of sum into a register, add val, and then push the result into the variable back. Thus, the line of code might be rewritten using pseudo code.

```
1   register.load(sum)
2   register.add(val)
3   register.write(sum)
```

As you can see, this is a non-atomic sequence of operations. Between two of them, the CPU might perform something else.

Let's assume sum has a value of 0. And we have two threads, adding a value each. Thread 1 might add 5, while thread 2 adds 3. The following sequence produces the expected result:

Operation	Result
Thread 1 register1.load(sum)	register1 = 0
Thread 1 register1.add(5)	register1 = 5
Thread 1 register1.write(sum)	sum = 5
Thread 2 register2.load(sum)	register2 = 5
Thread 2 register2.add(3)	register2 = 8
Thread 2 register2.write(sum)	sum = 8

But as both threads run independently, we cannot determine the execution order. At a different run, the statements might be executed in following order:

Operation	Result
Thread 1 register1.load(sum)	register1 = 0
Thread 1 register1.add(5)	register1 = 5
Thread 2 register2.load(sum)	register2 = 0 (sum is still 0 at this time!)
Thread 1 register1.write(sum)	sum = 5
Thread 2 register2.add(3)	register2 = 3
Thread 2 register2.write(sum)	sum = 3

What we've seen is a typical race condition. The result depends on which thread leads the race to the common variable. The method sum() became a critical section within the code. Such a section must be protected, for example, by a lock. Or you may use Java's qualifier synchronized.

```
public synchronized void sum(long val)
```

Now this method will be automatically protected. Only one thread at one time is allowed to run this method, whereas other threads are forced to wait. All the calls to sum() become serial, which destroys the parallelism. This can't be an appropriate solution.

VOLATILE

Maybe you have heard about the volatile qualifier for variables in a multithreaded environment and guess this would be a good choice. Sadly, this does not help. Volatile only guarantees that any read after a write will retrieve the last written value. Take a look at the first thread sequence, and there especially at Thread 2 register2.load(sum). The sum had been written in the step just before that. The former value had been 0. What happens if the read access would query the cache? Although just the 5 has been pushed to the var, Java might read the former 0. Volatile avoids this problem due to its guarantee: nothing more. Thus, volatile won't help (without we might have additional faults).

For more information, read about the Java Memory Model.[2]

Probably the best solution for our problem is to avoid the critical section. To avoid the shared variable, we simply create a separate SummingUnit for each thread. Each thread would solve a part of our problem—create a subtotal. At the end, we have to combine all of them.

The following is an example of parallel summing—with a separate SummingUnit for each thread:

```
1   public static void main(String[] args) throws
    InterruptedException {
2     List<Long> numbers = Utils.createNumbers();
3     int size = numbers.size();
4     SummingUnit summingUnit = new SummingUnit();
5     SummingUnit summingUnit2 = new SummingUnit();
6
7     Thread thread = new Thread(new SumTask(numbers, 0,
8             size / 2, summingUnit));
9     thread.start();
10
```

---

[2]https://www.cs.umd.edu/~pugh/java/memoryModel/jsr-133-faq.html

```
11      SumTask sumTask = new SumTask(numbers, size / 2,
12              size, summingUnit2);
13      sumTask.run();
14      thread.join(); // wait for thread to complete
15
16      summingUnit.combine(summingUnit2);
17      System.out.println("Sum: " + summingUnit.getSum());
18    }
```

In line 5 of the preceding code, a second SummingUnit is created, which is used in line 12. Then (line 16), the subtotals are combined. Because every thread uses its own object, we can avoid any synchronization.

Collect

After this short journey into Java concurrency, we'll come back to parallel streams and the collect() method. The mentioned overload taking three parameters is defined as

```
1    <R> R collect(Supplier<R> supplier,
2                   BiConsumer<R, ? super T> accumulator,
3                   BiConsumer<R, R> combiner);
```

The first parameter takes a function, which supplies a new result container of type R. We use a SummingUnit for R.

The accumulator parameter is a function that takes a result container R—which is a SummingUnit—and an object of the stream from type T. In our example, this is one of the numbers.

And the last parameter takes a function where Java passes two result containers in. This function performs the combination.

Putting all this together, we use SummingUnit within collect (Listing 10-6).

Listing 10-6. Using SummingUnit Within Collect

```
1  System.out.println("total: " +
2    numbers.parallelStream().collect(
3      () -> new SummingUnit(),      // supplier
4      (summingUnit, value) ->
5        summingUnit.sum(value),     // accumulator
6      (summingUnit, other) ->
7        summingUnit.combine(other) // combiner
8    ).getSum()
9  );
```

Now, if you run the program, you may recognize that the app prints out a couple of instances of "ctor SummingUnit." Remember, we print this within SummingUnit's constructor. This indicates that Java invokes a couple of threads to perform the work. In fact, Java uses the fork/join framework to schedule the threads. The principle of this framework is whether the task is small enough to run serial. If bigger, then the problem would be divided (best in two similar big parts), and both parts would be processed in different threads. Therefore, this algorithm is applied recursively.

If you're interested in more details about the fork/join framework, please refer to the Java Tutorials.[3]

As explained before, you can freely choose the names for lambda parameters. The scope is quite narrow. Thus, usually short names are chosen.

```
1  .collect(() -> new SummingUnit(),
2  (s, v) -> s.sum(v), (s, o) -> s.combine(o))
```

Alternatively we can use method references.

```
1  .collect(SummingUnit::new, SummingUnit::sum,
   SummingUnit::combine)
```

---

[3]https://docs.oracle.com/javase/tutorial/essential/concurrency/forkjoin.html

As the preceding examples show, it is quite easy to collect data. Usually it is not worthwhile to run such a simple task in parallel, but it should be no problem to transfer the knowledge to a more sophisticated task of your technical domain. Longer running tasks especially take profit from parallelism.

Instead of passing a couple of functions to the `collect()` method, we can write a Collector, which is passed to `collect()`. The following is the signature of the overloaded method:

```
1   <R, A> R collect(Collector<? super T, A, R> collector);
```

Collector is an interface we have to implement. We create a class *SummingCollector*, which returns the sum as a final result.

```
1   System.out.println("total: " +
2                numbers.parallelStream().collect(new
            SummingCollector()));
```

The Collector interface forces us to override a couple of methods that return functions. With lambdas, it's quite easy to define functions we can pass around as arguments. Besides (surprise!) supplier, accumulator, and combiner, we need to override the finisher. The finisher takes the last remaining result container for further processing. Our collector would return the final sum.

To reuse most of the code we have developed so far, the SummingCollector would internally delegate most tasks to a SummingUnit.

A last method we need to override returns a set of characteristics (Listing 10-7).

Listing 10-7. SummingCollector

```
1   public class SummingCollector
2                implements Collector<Long, SummingUnit,
            Long>{
3       @Override
```

```
4    public Supplier<SummingUnit> supplier() {
5      return () -> new SummingUnit();
6    }
7
8    @Override
9    public BiConsumer<SummingUnit, Long> accumulator() {
10     return (s, v) -> s.sum(v);
11   }
12
13   @Override
14   public BinaryOperator<SummingUnit> combiner() {
15     return (left, right) -> {left.combine(right); return
       left;};
16   }
17
18   @Override
19   public Function<SummingUnit, Long> finisher() {
20     return s -> s.getSum();
21   }
22
23   @Override
24   public Set<Characteristics> characteristics() {
25     return EnumSet.of(Characteristics.UNORDERED);
26     // do not add ", Characteristics.CONCURRENT"!
27   }
```

We parameterize the interface Collector with three types <T, A, R> as shown in the signature. Here T is Long (a number), A is replaced by a SummingUnit, and the result type R in the end is a Long too: the final sum.

Because we did *not* return the characteristic CONCURRENT, the supplier function is called for every thread. You may watch this by observing the output during object construction.

If we provide the characteristic CONCURRENT, Java assumes the supplier to be enabled for multithreading. It would create only one SummingUnit, which is shared by all the threads. And guess, the result would differ from run to run because we have a critical section with a race condition.

Summary

In this chapter we discussed the principles of a collector. The example showed, how a collector might be implemented. The parallel version of stream is very simple to use and hides all the painful stuff of threading, locking, synchronizing. But, a slightly knowledge of Java's concurrency features and typical problems like racing conditions is helpful to write a correct collector.

Final thoughts

Although this example had been very useful to discuss some aspects of parallelizm, it is not a real world example for a couple of reasons:

a. There is no need to implement a summing function because Java offers one out of the box

```
numbers.parallelStream().mapToLong(i -> i).sum();
```

Internally Java implements the sum using the „dirty" trick with an array to hold a simple value.

b. Instead of collecting data, we may simply reduce the data.

```
numbers.parallelStream().reduce(0L, (a, c) ->
a + c);
```

The reduce function creates a new object with every addition. It starts with zero. Then it takes two arguments, the accumulator and the current object. It returns the sum of both which is stored as a new object into the accumulator. Because there is no shared object, we do not have shared state, no race condition etc.

But sometimes we really need a collector, for example if we want to collect objects into a collection or map. This is shown in the next chapter.

Grouping Collector

Let's assume we want to calculate the average spending of persons, grouped by age. We want to create a collector that returns a Map<Integer, Double> in which the Integer represents the age group and the Double represents average spendings.

To verify this collector, we use a simple output:

Listing 11-1. Preparing the output

```
1   [. . .]
2
3   [ommited: create persons as shown before]
4
5   printResults(persons.getPersons().parallelStream()
6     .collect(new GroupAverageCollector()));
7
8   [. . .]
9
```

© Michael Müller 2016
M. Müller, *Java Lambdas and Parallel Streams*,
DOI 10.1007/978-1-4842-2487-8_11

```
10   private static void printResults(Map<Integer, Double>
     results) {
11     System.out.println("");
12     for (int group : results.keySet()) {
13       System.out.println("Group: " + group + ";  avg: " +
       results.get(group));
14     }
15   }
```

Remember the data structure introduced at the beginning of this book. All of the persons contain a list of buyings. The prices are internally stored at cents to avoid floating point operations. To keep the collector lean, we use a helping class that sums up the cents and the person count and calculates the average = sum(cents) / 100 / personCount.

Listing 11-2. *Helper class to calculate the average*

```
1    public class AverageBuilder {
2
3      private int _count;
4      private long _cents;
5
6      public int getCount() {
7        return _count;
8      }
9
10     public long getCents() {
11       return _cents;
12     }
13
14     public void add(long cents) {
15       _count++;
16       _cents += cents;
17     }
18
19     public void add(AverageBuilder other) {
20       _count += other.getCount();
21       _cents += other.getCents();
22     }
23
```

```
24    public double getAverage() {
25      return _cents / 100D / _count;
26    }
27  }
```

This class contains two add methods: one to add the spendings of one person and the second to combine two AverageBuilders.

In Chapter 10, we started with a SummingUnit, which was reused within the collector. The collector we use in this chapter is not based on such an existing class. Instead, it contains the functions to accumulate, combine, and finish:

Listing 11-3. GroupAverageCollector implementing accumulator, combiner, and finisher

```
1   public class GroupAverageCollector implements
2       Collector<Person, Map<Integer, AverageBuilder>,
        Map<Integer, Double>> {
3
4     @Override
5     public Supplier<Map<Integer, AverageBuilder>>
      supplier() {
6       return () -> new HashMap<>();
7     }
8
9     @Override
10    public BiConsumer<Map<Integer, AverageBuilder>,
      Person> accumulator() {
11      return (m, p) -> add(m, p);
12    }
13
14    @Override
15    public BinaryOperator<Map<Integer, AverageBuilder>>
      combiner() {
16      return (left, right) -> {
17        combine(left, right);
18        return left;
19      };
20    }
21
```

```
22    @Override
23    public Function<Map<Integer, AverageBuilder>,
      Map<Integer, Double>> finisher() {
24      return m -> finish(m);
25    }
26
27    @Override
28    public Set<Characteristics> characteristics() {
29      return EnumSet.of(Characteristics.UNORDERED);
30      // no Characteristics.CONCURRENT!
31    }
32
33    private static void add(Map<Integer, AverageBuilder>
      map, Person person) {
34      int group = person.getAge() / 10;
35      if (!map.containsKey(group)) {
36        map.put(group, new AverageBuilder());
37      }
38      long cents = person.getBuying().values()
39              .stream().mapToLong(a -> a.getAmount().
                getCents()).sum();
40      map.get(group).add(cents);
41    }
42
43    private static void combine(Map<Integer,
      AverageBuilder> left,
44            Map<Integer, AverageBuilder> right) {
45      for (int group : right.keySet()) {
46        if (!left.containsKey(group)) {
47          left.put(group, right.get(group));
48        } else {
49          left.get(group).add(right.get(group));
50        }
51      }
52    }
53
54    private static Map<Integer, Double>
      finish(Map<Integer, AverageBuilder> map) {
55      Map<Integer, Double> result = new HashMap<>();
56      for (int group : map.keySet()) {
57        result.put(group, map.get(group).getAverage());
58      }
```

```
59      return result;
60   }
61
62 }
```

Line 2. This collector takes object of type Person. It accumulates the values in a Map<Integer, AverageBuilder> and returns a Map<Integer, Double>.

Line 6. The supplier produces a new HashMap for every thread because there is no Characteristics.CONCURRENT.

Line 11. Remember accumulator, combiner, and finisher do not return values but pointers to the functions that are implemented within this collector as static functions (methods).

Line 3. In this example, the age groups are simply calculated by an integer division.

Line 39. All buyings are stored within a list. We use a stream to sum up the cents.

The combine function merges two maps into one, and the finish function transforms the intermediate result into the required output format. All functions shall be understandable to you as a Java developer.

Because we did not use Characteristics.CONCURRENT, the stream framework creates a new map per thread. Although processed in parallel, the functions are implemented as in the good old days of simple sequential programming.

What would happen if we use Characteristics.CONCURRENT? Before you continue reading, please think about this. Hopefully you'll recognize all the implications.

(Take some time to think about it)

As mentioned before, the framework will call the supplier only once. It creates one map, which is used within all threads. First of all, a HashMap is not a thread save. This can be solved easily by replacing it with a ConcurrentHashMap. But if you run the program, you'll get non-deterministic results.

The add methods is a critical section. It might be interrupted at any time. And it contains a shared state. Both might result in false values as described in Chapter 10. A simple solution is to make the add synchronized:

Listing 11-4. Critical section protected by synchronized

```
1    private static synchronized void add(Map<Integer,
2                    AverageBuilder> map, Person person) {...}
```

Because synchronization slows down the performance, this usually is not a good choice.

Summary

In this chapter, I discussed a collector that really "collects" data. Depending on the design and the characteristics of the collector, special multithreaded handling might be avoided. Thus, parallel programming without explicit synchronization, locking, and so forth is prevalent possible. But a basic knowledge of multithreading pitfalls is necessary to create sequential-alike programs that fit well in a parallel processing environment.

Final Thoughts

The intention of this compact book is to show you the principles of Java lambdas and parallel streams. It does not explain every detail such as every intermediate or final operator. With the knowledge of its principles, it should be no problem to understand these operations by exploring the API documentation. One good starting point is the documentation of the package java.util.stream (https://docs.oracle.com/javase/8/docs/api/index.html?java/util/stream/package-summary.html).

One last tip to start your journey: A great way to learn how to use streams is to do it interactively. Java 9 comes with an interactive shell that is great for this purpose. As of the time of this writing, Java 9 is available as an early access version (https://jdk9.java.net). I irregularly blog about this shell (http://blog.mueller-bruehl.de). The main article so far is "Interactive Java with jshell" (http://blog.mueller-bruehl.de/netbeans/interactive-java-with-jshell).

Now it is time to let you explore the great world of lambdas and streams by yourself. I hope this book was quite interesting, understandable, and valuable to you. Let me know!

Program to Create the Demo Data

To perform the analysis mentioned in this book, you need some demo data. This data was created with a program that is shown on the next pages. This software was developed with a quick generation in mind and not for educational purposes. In this respect, it is kept more simple than pedagogically valuable.

© Michael Müller 2016
M. Müller, *Java Lambdas and Parallel Streams*,
DOI 10.1007/978-1-4842-2487-8

Basic Data

The program needs some basic information to create the data. This data is stored in four CSV comma separated values) files (Listing A-1 through A-4).

Listing A-1. *Surnames.csv*

```
1   Andersson
2   Angelopoulos
3   Athanasiadis
4   Bakker
5   Bauer
6   Beck
7   Becker
8   Bernard
9   Bianchi
10  Borg
11  [...]Demo dataSurnames.csv
```

Listing A-2. *GivenNamesFemale.csv*

```
1   Aadhya
2   Aisha
3   Aline
4   Amelia
5   Ananya
6   Anette
7   Anika
8   Anja
9   Antje
10  Ashraqat
11  [...]
```

Listing A-3. *GivenNamesMale.csv*

```
1   Adam
2   Ahmet
3   Ali
4   Andreas
5   Aron
6   Ben
7   Bilal
```

```
·8   Bram
 9   Charlie
10   Christoph
11   [...]
```

Listing A-4. Articles.csv

```
 1   CarSmall;15000;1;5
 2   CarBig;80000;1;3
 3   Bred;2.5;5;1000
 4   Water;0.3;10;1000
 5   Shirt;20;3;100
 6   Butter;3;5;250
 7   Milk;0.7;5;500
 8   Book;30;5;80
 9   Beer;1.5;10;600
10   Potatoes;1.90;10;900
11   [...]Demo dataArticles.csv
```

Whereas the first three files only contain names, a little explanation is needed for the articles. Each article consists of four columns:

- name
- price
- maximum amount per buying
- buying probability

This (fictitious) data is used to simulate a kind of "realistic" purchase behavior. For example, a car costs much more than milk. On the other hand, people usually buy milk more often and in bigger quantities.

Article

Each line of the file `Articles.csv` will be passed to the constructor of the class `Article`. The line will be split into the four values and assigned to the internal attributes. Besides that, each article is defined by an article number, which is assigned during data creation. Unlike in productive software, we assume all data to be correct. Thus, no checks are implemented for this demo.

ℹ️ For brevity, `package` and `import` directives are omitted in the following classes (Listing A-5). Required imports will be automatically added by a modern IDE. Using NetBeans, for example, you may perform this task by pressing {Ctrl+Shift+I}.

Listing A-5. Article.java

```
1   public class Article {
2
3     private final int _articleNo;
4     private String _name;
5     private Money _price;
6     private int _maxSell;
7     private int _probability;
8
9     public Article(String articleData, int articleNo) {
10      _articleNo = articleNo;
11      try {
12        String[] parts = articleData.split(";");
13        _name = parts[0];
14        _price = new Money(parts[1]);
15        _maxSell = Integer.parseInt(parts[2]);
16        _probability = Integer.parseInt(parts[3]);
17      } catch (NumberFormatException e) {
18        System.out.println(e.getMessage());
19        throw e;
20      }
21    }
22
23    public String getName() {
24      return _name;
25    }
26
27    public void setName(String name) {
28      _name = name;
29    }
30
```

```
31      public Money getPrice() {
32        return _price;
33      }
34
35      public void setPrice(Money price) {
36        _price = price;
37      }
38
39      public int getMaxSells() {
40        return _maxSell;
41      }
42
43      public void setMaxSell(int maxSell) {
44        _maxSell = maxSellArticle.java;
45      }
46
47      public int getProbability() {
48        return _probability;
49      }
50
51      public void setProbability(int probability) {
52        _probability = probability;
53      }
54
55    }
```

In line 5 of Listing A-5, the variable _price is declared with a type of Money. This class will be shown in the following. Besides that, the class mainly consists of getters and setters.

If articles will be bought or sold, this will be stored for the article with amount and price. The price can't be derived by amount * single price because it might be altered due to a discount.

This information is stored in *ArticleInfo* (Listing A-6).

Listing A-6. ArticleInfo.java

```
1   public class ArticleInfo {
2     private final int _articleNo;
3     private long _quantity;
4     private Money _amount;
5
6     public ArticleInfo (int articleNo){
7       _articleNo = articleNo;
8       _amount = new Money();
9     }
10    public int getArticleNo() {
11      return _articleNo;
12    }
13
14    public long getQuantity() {
15      return _quantity;
16    }
17
18    public void setQuantity(long quantity) {
19      _quantity = quantity;
20    }
21
22    public Money getAmount() {
23      return _amount;
24    }
25
26    public void setAmount(Money amount) {
27      _amount = amountArticleInfo.java;
28    }
29
30    public void addQuantity (long quantity){
31      _quantity += quantity;
32    }
33    public void addPrice(long cents){
34      _amount.add(cents);
35    }
36  }
```

Persons

Within the class Person, not only name and age, but also buyings—and (in case of vendor) sellings—are stored (Listing A-7). For the latter, a ConcurrentHashMap is used (instead of a simple HashMap). This is one of the little prerequisites for parallelism (see the description in the text).

Listing A-7. Person.java

```
1    public class Person {
2
3      private String _givenName;
4      private String _surname;
5      private Gender _gender;
6      private int _age;
7      private Map<Integer, ArticleInfo> _selling = new
         ConcurrentHashMap<>();
8      private Map<Integer, ArticleInfo> _buying = new
         ConcurrentHashMap<>();
9      private int _discount;
10
11     public String getGivenName() {
12       return _givenName;
13     }
14
15     public void setGivenName(String givenName) {
16       _givenName = givenName;
17     }
18
19     public String getSurname() {
20       return _surname;
21     }
22
23     public void setSurname(String surname) {
24       _surname = surname;
25     }
```

```
26
27    public Gender getGender() {
28      return _gender;
29    }
30
31    public void setGender(Gender gender) {
32      _gender = genderPerson.java;
33    }
34
35    public boolean isFemale(){
36      return _gender == Gender.Female;
37    }
38
39    public int getAge() {
40      return _age;
41    }
42
43    public void setAge(int age) {
44      _age = age;
45    }
46
47    public boolean isVendor() {
48      return _selling.size() > 0;
49    }
50
51    public int getDiscount() {
52      return _discount;
53    }
54
55    public void setDiscount(int discount) {
56      _discount = discount;
57    }
58
59    public Map<Integer, ArticleInfo> getSelling() {
60      return _sellingPerson.java;
61    }
62
63    public void setSelling(Map<Integer, ArticleInfo>
      selling) {
64      _selling = selling;
65    }
66
```

```
67    public Map<Integer, ArticleInfo> getBuying() {
68      return _buying;
69    }
70
71    public void setBuying(Map<Integer, ArticleInfo>
      buying) {
72      _buying = buying;
73    }
74
75  }
```

All these persons are kept in an instance of the class Persons. This class also contains some features to create all the persons (Listing A-8).

Listing A-8. Persons.java

```
1   public class Persons {
2
3     private final static int PersonCount = 50000;
4     private final Random _random = new SecureRandom();
5     private final static Persons _instance = new
      Persons();
6     private final List<Person> _persons = new
      ArrayList<>();
7
8     public List<Person> getPersons() {
9       return _persons;
10    }
11
12    private final List<Person> _sellers = new
      ArrayList<>();
13
14    private Persons() {
15      for (int i = 0; i < PersonCount; i++) {
16        Person person = createPerson();
17        _persons.add(person);
18        if (person.isVendor()) {
19          _sellers.add(person)Persons.java;
20        }
21      }
22      long maxSells = PersonCount * (50 + _random.
      nextInt(50));
```

```
23        for (int i = 0; i <= maxSells; i++) {
24          trySell();
25        }
26      }
27
28      public static Persons getInstance() {
29        return _instance;
30      }
31
32      private Person createPerson() {
33        Person person = new Person();
34        List<String> surNames = DataProvider.getInstance().
          getSurNames();
35        person.setSurname(surNames.get(_random.
          nextInt(surNames.size())));
36        Map<String, Gender> givenNameInfos = DataProvider.
          getInstance()
37            .getGivenNames();
38        List<String> givenNames = givenNameInfos.keySet()
39              .stream().collect(Collectors.toList());
40        person.setGivenName(givenNames.get(_random.
          nextInt(givenNames.size())));
41        person.setGender(givenNameInfos.get(person.
          getGivenName()));
42        person.setAge(15 + _random.nextInt(80));
43        if (_random.nextInt(100) == 0) {
44          makeVendor(person);
45        }
46        return person;
47      }
48
49      private void makeVendor(Person person) {
50        person.setDiscount(_random.nextInt(5) * 5);
51        Map<Integer, ArticleInfo> selling = person.
          getSelling()Persons.java;
52
53        for (int i = 0; i <= _random.nextInt(10); i++) {
54          int articleNo = 1 + _random.nextInt(DataProvider.
            getInstance()
55                .getArticles().size());
56          if (selling.containsKey(articleNo)) {
57            break;
```

```
58        }
59        selling.put(articleNo, new ArticleInfo(articleNo));
60      }
61    }
62
63    private void trySell() {
64      Person seller = _sellers.get(_random.nextInt(_
          sellers.size()));
65      assert (seller != null);
66      Person buyer = _persons.get(_random.nextInt(_
          persons.size()));
67      assert (buyer != null);
68      if (seller == buyer) {
69        return;
70      }
71      Map<Integer, ArticleInfo> selling = seller.
          getSelling();
72      Map<Integer, ArticleInfo> buying = buyer.
          getBuying();
73      Object[] articleNumbers = selling.keySet().
          toArray();
74      int index = _random.nextInt(articleNumbers.length);
75      int articleNo = (int) articleNumbers[index];
76      Article article = DataProvider.getInstance()
77              .getArticles().get(articleNo);
78
79      if (_random.nextInt(1000) < article.
          getProbability()
80                                  + seller.getDiscount() /
                                    5)Persons.java {
81        int quantity = 1 + _random.nextInt(article.
          getMaxSells());
82        long price = quantity * article.getPrice().
          getCents()
83                    * (100 - seller.getDiscount()) / 100;
84        ArticleInfo infoSelling = selling.get(articleNo);
85        infoSelling.setQuantity(infoSelling.getQuantity()
          + quantity);
86        infoSelling.getAmount().add(price);
87        ArticleInfo infoBuying = buying.
          containsKey(articleNo)
88                ? buying.get(articleNo)
```

```
89                    : new ArticleInfo(articleNo);
90          infoBuying.addQuantity(quantity);
91          infoBuying.addPrice(price)Persons.java;
92          buying.put(articleNo, infoBuying);
93        }
94      }
95    }
```

Other Classes

Listing A-9. *Gender.java*

```
1   public enum Gender {
2       Male,
3       Female;
4   }
```

The amount of money consists of Euro and Cent (Dollar and Cent, …). Floats or Doubles have problems representing such accurate data. are too cumbersome for our requirement. For the demonstration of Lambdas and Streams, a simple class Money was created, which internally stores all the amounts using Cents (see Listing A-10). Thus, it can calculate with Integers (more precise *long* values).

Listing A-10. *Money.java*

```
1   public class Money {
2
3     private long _cents;
4
5     Money() {
6       _cents = 0;
7     }
8
9     Money(String value) {
10      setValue(value);
11    }
12
13    public long getCents() {
14      return _cents;
15    }
```

```
16
17      public void setCents(long cents) {
18        _cents = cents;
19      }
20
21      public String getValue() {
22        return _cents / 100 + "." + _cents % 100;
23      }
24
25      public void setValue(String value) {
26        int pos = value.indexOf(".");
27        if (pos == -1) {
28          _cents = 100 * Long.parseLong(value);
29        } else {
30          _cents = 100 * Long.parseLong(value.substring(0,
            pos));
31          String decimals = value.substring(pos + 1) + "00";
32          _cents += Long.parseLong(decimals.substring(0, 2));
33        }
34      }
35
36      public void add (long cents){
37        _cents += centsMoney.java;
38      }
39    }
```

The DataProvider is used to read the sample data out of the four files (Listing A-11).

Listing A-11. DataProvider.java

```
1    public class DataProvider {
2
3      private static final DataProvider _instance = new
         DataProvider();
4      private List<String> _surNames = new ArrayList<>();
5      private final Map<String, Gender> _givenNames = new
         HashMap<>();
6      private final Map<Integer, Article> _articles = new
         HashMap<>();
7
8      public static DataProvider getInstance() {
9        return _instance;
10     }
```

```
11
12      private DataProvider() {
13        init();
14      }
15
16      public List<String> getSurNames() {
17        return _surNames;
18      }
19
20      public Map<String, Gender> getGivenNames() {
21        return _givenNames;
22      }
23
24      public Map<Integer, Article> getArticles() {
25        return _articles;
26      }
27
28      private void init() {
29        try {
30          _surNames = readFile("Surnames.csv");
31          readFile("GivenNamesFemale.csv").stream()
32                      .forEach(n -> _givenNames.put(n,
                          Gender.Female));
33          readFile("GivenNamesMale.csv").stream()
34                      .forEach(n -> _givenNames.put(n,
                          Gender.Male));
35          int articleNo = 0;
36          for (String line : readFile("Articles.csv")) {
37            if (!line.trim().isEmpty()) {
38              articleNo++;
39              Article article = new Article(line,
                  articleNo);
40              _articles.put(articleNo, article);
41            }
42          };
43        } catch (IOException ex) {
44          Logger.getLogger(DataProvider.class.getName())
45                      .log(Level.SEVERE, null, ex);
46        }
47      }DataProvider.java
48
49      private List<String> readFile(String fileName) throws
        IOException {
```

```
50      List<String> lines = new ArrayList<>();
51      try (InputStream is = getClass().
        getResourceAsStream(fileName);
52              BufferedReader reader = new
                BufferedReader(new InputStreamReader\
53   (is));) {
54          String line;
55          while ((line = reader.readLine()) != null) {
56              lines.add(line);
57          }
58      }
59      return linesDataProvider.java;
60   }
61 }
```

Demo Program

The following main method shows how to call the data generation and to perform an analysis (see Listing A-12). You may use this skeleton to execute your own experiments with Lambdas and Streams.

Listing A-12. StreamsDemo.java

```
1    public class StreamsDemo {
2
3      public static void main(String[] args) {
4        System.out.println("started");
5        Persons persons = Persons.getInstance();
6        System.out.println("created " + persons.
         getPersons().size()
7                            + " persons.");
8
9        showAverage(persons.getPersons());
10
11       [... many other show cases ...]
12     }
13
14     private static void showAverage(List<Person> persons)
{
15         double averageAge = persons.stream()
```

```
16                    .filter(p -> p.getAge() < 20 &&
                      p.isFemale())
17                    .mapToInt(Person::getAge)
18                    .average()
19                    .getAsDouble();
20        System.out.println("averageAge: " + averageAge);
21      }
22    }
```

The source code for this demo is available at webdevelop-
ment-java.info.[1]

---

[1]http://webdevelopment-java.info

I

Index

A

Anonymous classes, 11–12
API documentation, 26
ArticleInfo.java, 73
Article.java, 72
Articles.csv, 71
AverageBuilders, 63

B

Behavior parameterization, 9–10

C

Central processing unit (CPU), 48
class Money, 80
collect() method, 31, 47
    characteristic
        CONCURRENT, 59
    function, 56
    lambda parameters, 57
    overload, 56
    SummingCollector, 58–59
    SummingUnit, 58

    technical domain, 58
    types, 59
Collector and concurrency
    Java concurrency, 48
    number generator, 48
ConcurrentHashMap, 65
ctor SummingUnit, 57

D, E

Data
    sales and purchases, 5
    structure, 5
DataProvider.java, 81–83
Data transformation, 29
Default methods
    binary compatibility, 19
    "homonymous" methods, 20
    interface, 19
    Java virtual, 20–21
    rules, 21–24
Demo data
    Articles.csv, 70–71
    columns, 71

© Michael Müller 2016
M. Müller, *Java Lambdas and Parallel Streams*,
DOI 10.1007/978-1-4842-2487-8

Demo data (*cont.*)
    CSV comma, 69–71
    GivenNamesFemale.csv, 70
    GivenNamesMale.csv, 70
    Surnames.csv, 70

F

Filter, 8
Functional interface, 14–15

G

get(), 26–27
getAsDouble(), 27
GroupingCollector
    average spending, 61
    characteristics, 65
    data structure, 62
    functions, 63
    interactive shell, 67
    Java developer, 65
    output, 61
    Person, 65
    person count, 62
    shared state, 66
    stream framework, 65
    streams, 67
    synchronization, 66

H

HashMap, 65, 75
hasNext(), 39

I

Integer, 61

J, K

Java concurrency, 45
    calculation, 51
    class, 50

combine(), 51
CPU, 53
execution order, 54
intermediate operations, 49
Java's qualifier, 54
parallel streams, 48–49
parallel summing, 52–53
parameters, 52
sequence, 53
syntactic sugar, 53
technical class, 50
usage of thread, 50
Java Development Kit (JDK), 49
Java lambdas, 66

L

Lambda expressions
    condition interface, 14
    execution time, 17
    female persons, 14
    Java 8, 13
    measuring method, 18
Lambdas, 67
    expressions, 41
    notation, 16–17
Lambdas and (parallel) streams, 1–3
Language Integrated Query, 1

M

.mapToLong(…)), 37
method get()
Money.java, 80

N

Null value, 25

O

Optional class, 25–26
OptionalDouble, 26

OptionalInt, 26
OptionalLong, 26
Optional<T>, 38
orElse(), 26

P, Q

parallel(), 43
Parallel processing, 33–34
Parallel programming, 66
Parallel stream, 2, 34, 36, 148
  binary Function, 44
  calculation, 43
  demonstration, 44
  elements, 42
  functional programming, 42
  lambda expressions., 41
  processing, 42
  programming, 44
  sequential variant, 43
Parameterization, 8–11
Person.java, 75, 77
person.stream(), 31
Pipelining, 29–30

R

reduce() method, 47
run() method, 50

S

someCondition(), 33
someOther-Condition(), 33
Spliterator, 34
  hasNext(), 39
  implementation, 39

next()., 39
threads, 38
tryAdvance, 39
trySplit, 39
start() method, 50
stream(), 36
Stream
  lambda expression, 37
  mapToLong(...)), 37
Stream prosessing
  ancillary conditions, 34
  calculation, 32
  collected into a list, 31
  concrete solution, 32
  explicit intermediate
    result, 30
  intermediate operation, 33
  internal iterator, 30
  mapping, 31
  process chain, 33
  single processing steps, 31
  termediate from terminal
    operations., 32
  traditional approach, 32
  variation, 31
  vendors, 32
StreamsDemo.java, 83–84
StreamSupport.stream, 36
SummingUnit, 51, 55–57

T, U

Target list, 8

V, W, X, Y, Z

variable _price, 73

Get the eBook for only $4.99!

Why limit yourself?

Now you can take the weightless companion with you wherever you go and access your content on your PC, phone, tablet, or reader.

Since you've purchased this print book, we are happy to offer you the eBook for just $4.99.

Convenient and fully searchable, the PDF version enables you to easily find and copy code—or perform examples by quickly toggling between instructions and applications.

To learn more, go to http://www.apress.com/us/shop/companion or contact support@apress.com.

Printed in the United States
By Bookmasters